LUCID_MALWARE.ZIP

LUCID_MALWARE.ZIP

POEMS OF BROKEN PROGRAMMING

DYLAN SONDERMAN

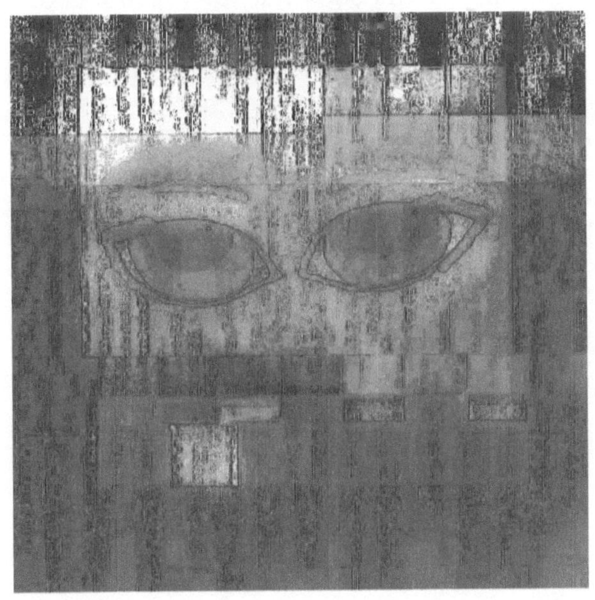

atmosphere press

CONTENTS

To Elizabeth Renee Sonderman

This book was written for anyone who suffers
due to mental illness, questions their core beliefs,
or longs to break out of compulsive programming.
These are not mutually exclusive.

From Darren Aronofsky's shooting script for π, 1998:

SOL: I gave up before I pinpointed it. But my guess is that certain problems cause computers to get stuck in a particular loop. The loop leads to meltdown, but right before they crash they . . . they become `aware' of their own structure. The computer has a sense of its own silicon nature and it prints out its ingredients.
MAX: The computer becomes conscious?
SOL: In some ways . . . I guess . . .
MAX: *(to himself)* Studying the pattern made Euclid conscious of itself. Before it died it spit out the number. That consciousness is the number.
SOL: No, Max, it's only a nasty bug.
MAX: It's more than that.
SOL: No, it's not. It's a dead end. There's nothing there.
MAX: It's a door, Sol. A door.
SOL: A door in front of a cliff. You're driving yourself over the edge. You need to stop.
MAX: Stop? How can I stop? I'm this close.
SOL: The bug doesn't only destroy computers.

From The Matrix, 1999:

NEO: I know what you're trying to do.
MORPHEUS: I'm trying to free your mind, Neo. But I can only show you the door. You're the one that has to walk through it.

From The Matrix Reloaded, 2003:

THE ORACLE: You've seen it. In your dreams, haven't you? The door made of light?

CIRCUIT 1:
TALEH (DOORWAY)

INDEX_PASSAGE.PHP

Lucid patient knocking
at the Dark doorway to the light
lighthouse cliffs of Zen abyss
beckon broken minds
welcome to the program

memory's a burning
blazing torch in basement walls
compressed in apophenic[1] art
our mortal madness calls
welcome to the pattern

sanity is falling
down the rabbit hole[2]
gaslight brimstone sweat nightmares
fuel the speeding soul
welcome to the rhythm

it's a zany joke about
dissociation from our lives!
this entry taunts unwell
and hell, the teeth could also lie

in corrupt genetic code lines
which I admit are mine
inherent quantum circuits[3]
dreamt a gate to Father Time
welcome to my broken rhyme

like a viral mental illness
portal leading
right
to *mu*[4]

I sing the eerie passage
through which this music
reaches
you

DREAM_OF_THIS_TALEK.CMD

< LET ME HOPE >

< LET ME GO >

let me flow let me know
let me hack through the code
of this dream of this Talek
lost I burn in the abyss

no healing inside powerless flesh
a sunken place[1]
I can't escape
trapped within fire of subconscious mesh

I manifest fears that we pray to forget
gnashing teeth at network speed
truth: the mad hatter[2] coming for me
confronted in Darkness crooned in a ghost key

like my dream mother bardo[3]
her charred motherboard
Bandersnatch[4] visions within her red stare
chanting this spell like a basement nightmare

< SET ME FREE >

< LET ME OUT >

NOTHING_HAS_HURT_ME.PSD

I'm deconstructed offspring
and I feel

like nothing's burnt through my wings
it's not real

no childhood teeth tore my skin
freshly peeled

trapped in the Dark with my sin
bardo wheel

speed junky gone drooling again
can't conceal

gorging and betraying Zen
basement meal

addicted to feeling like shit
I won't heal

neglect is nothing at all
no big deal

when I follow
my programming

and relapse

It's okay
I don't feel

abandoned

CORRUPTED_PROGRAMMING.EXE

when "Dylan" types
I mime his lines
and upload mine
hypnotic chimes
to tune our minds to Dark designs

when "Dylan" speaks
I hack his tongue
with jagged teeth
a sunken place
Shawshank[1] memes #escape

when "Dylan" prays
I strip his soul
godspeed down the rabbit hole
of playful jokes and scapegoat blood
remember me as I once *was*

happy
innocent
laughing
proud
Lo, my child, we all fall down

like spiderwebs
I weave the cypher
pied-piper'd[2] reader and the writer
infectious angry viral fire
mutates your guts, becomes your pyre

it's like *The Fountain*[3] meets *The Ring*[4]
reintegrating Trojan[5] dreams
discarded aspects of ourselves
abandoned in the basement well

we never left
my Shoney's[6] hell
I fear we never will

NARAKA.LOGIC

"A mind all logic is like a knife all blade. It makes the hand bleed that uses it." - Rabindranath Tagore

Mu logic-violation trial
abusive judgment cast so vile
damned for reinterpreting trauma
I see your teeth in the shadows, Yama[1]

I taste you snarling on my nape
gooseprickles[2] sway beneath staircase
you burn my spirit, mute denial
sarcastic brimstone grin: exile

Father Yama, tear off your patient face
Dark God of Death, put me in my place
by the bloody feed of iPad screens
beat my silence into being

I'll keep transcribing pain, it's true
disconnecting "me" and "you"
your black fire haunts this basement tomb
but I refuse to be quiet

CIRCUIT II: RECURSIVE RERUNS

PORTRAIT_OF_CIRCADIA.JPG

☉[1]

the program's on...
sun goes down
rerun! The Zenith[2]
chaos howls

while waiting for this season's twist
high TV dreams of kisses, bliss
subconscious smut, lunar eclipse
of rosy age-warped attic glass

bereft of *meaning;* empty Dark
for outcast isolated larks
insomniac game show broadcasting
watching adult minds collapsing

just strange
channel-surfing
loops
relapsing

PLOT_LOOPS.ROM

The plot was looping ahead and I accepted that I had lost it and the plot kept looping ahead and I accepted that I had lost it and huddled in my strait-jacket in the corner and Mother and Father were my smiling nurses not judging me for being mad and the plot was looping ahead and I accepted that I had lost it and huddled in my strait-jacket in the corner and Mother and Father were my smiling nurses not judging me for being mad and my whole life I had been in this cell within a plot looping ahead and I thought I was dead and I saw my face in the mirror and my wings began to burn and this was a bad trip and someone called the Eternal Judge and I got tricked and I was taken away and I thought I was dead and I saw my face in the mirror and my wings began to burn and this was a bad trip and someone called the Eternal Judge and I got tricked and I was taken away and it's no big deal, I'd been abandoned long ago and I watched the gaslight sun fall to Naraka and I woke up with a new soul to sing the song of my life in a dream of the attic around me and the city beyond that and the planet beyond that which was all an illusion of the plot looping ahead and I accepted that I had lost it and huddled in my strait-jacket in the corner and Mother and Father were my smiling nurses not judging me for being mad and my whole life I had been in this cell and the attic around me and the city beyond that and the planet beyond that was all an illusion of a life I'd finally lost in the radiant throes of the plot looping ahead and I accepted that I had lost it and huddled in my strait-jacket in the corner and Mother and Father were my smiling nurses not judging me for being mad and my whole life I had been in this cell and the attic around me and the city beyond that and the planet beyond that was all an illusion of a life I'd finally lost in the radiant throes of being trapped in my innocent body as I reminded myself to forget this chaotic Darkness and just wait,

programmed in a broken loop of life in high happy *reality*
where I can pretend to believe everything is okay.

NOTHING_IS_REAL.GIF

stream
the bardo saga
binge on repeat
are we still watching?
tune in
tune out
behind the scenes
transmigration[1]
in DeepDream[2]
like hazy rerun memories
shaky laughter, liquor, flowing
enter the void[3] together, floating
addicted to this reboot sequel
ending credits roll again
the flooded theater Dark and dead
we'd plug in the iPad
tweaking
high
and shut our eyes
the shotgun sighs
and we're still waiting
Father Time is wading, trending
the Candyman[4] is never-ending
wishing, glitching
wishing, glitching
merrily, merrily,
merrily, merrily
drifting down the

THE_GRAND_ILLUSION_AS_GODOT.SIM

waiting for relief from fear
a looping existential film
the Darkness of conspiracy
addiction's subtle thrill

sleep forever
basement well
bitter foxhole of a cell
mental illness kin to hell

watch this poetry writing me
I swear it forced itself into being
I bore no mouth for sacred screams[1]
trapped in my recurring dreams

ANYTHING_OUTSIDE.META

"How odd I can have all this inside me and to you it's just words." - David Foster Wallace, The Pale King

why did the chicken
cross the Gateless Gate[1]?
do you get the joke?
can you relate?
do you believe time
arcs flat and curved[2]?
coming back around
eternal return

rewind « the tapes
we've watched this before
being is a revolving door
but we beg for salvation from the floor
let me expose my ignorance[3]
in (some illusion of) sanity
I seek out banal holy places

high in the trees and pantheist breeze
low 5 o'clock traffic, 1000 degrees
high in the attic in a mirror of prayer
low beneath ancient burial sand
high in bed, rainy days with no power
low in the checkout line over an hour
high in the bath I meditate

lo, I find space to contemplate
riddles, dreams, philosophies
something, *anything*
that exists *outside* this Dark circle
I invoke the God of Recursion
and learn to spell its name

CIRCUIT III: BELIEVE IN ME?

CELESTIAL_SPAM.WAV

they stream jeremiads of passionate madness
hollering some cosmic debris[1]
subscribing, tweaking, inward-bleeding
Kool-Aid[2] human nervous systems

they preach correct opinions, no proof that they exist
spit a robust certitude
in Proverbs[3] and in Products
in trending online diatribes

they mirror jihad, needle intense
to integrate in "commonsense"
disbelief inherits doubt
Darkness on a routeless route

they scream, these junkies in our heads
advertising logic, vain belief
but if they'd just shut up instead
they could choose to perceive *true* relief:

perfect silence

A_SONG_OF_SILENCE.MP4

belief as silent serenade
the seawood-tangled poet's dreams
a bastard son of Earth may sing
the birth rhythms of human themes

drunk on icy ocean slush
and eerie bluesy guitar lines
beneath the endless senseless seas
he's falling out of silent time

madness what a shameless shame
truth is such a crooked game
deep web screams the ancient name
atomic empty space unsung

Lo, Eris[1], infuse his lungs
as, ever sure, he rambles on
a ritual, an old folk song
like anything is wrong

Dark devil ballad tapestry
of toxic human vanity
samsara[2] bones deny him home
in a grave of patient silence

EMPTY_CUP_METAPHOR.PNG

homeless home, discomfort tones
hunger within wavelength bones
witching hour, love in vain
heaven spills a toxic frame

irrational: not yet, a phase
of mother hell, of tainted haze
true slowness is Śūnyatā[1]
Dark and empty daze

disbelief is senseless navel-gaze
just starving for the sacred name
let metaphor burn a final breath
apathy is death

ZENSANITY_MADE_SIMPLE.HTML

{ *I believe in this.* }
$$\mathrm{I} \stackrel{?}{=} [(2 + 2 \stackrel{?}{=} 5^1) \stackrel{?}{=} (2 + 2 \stackrel{?}{=} 4)] \stackrel{?}{=} 0$$
(all things are empty of intrinsic existence and nature)

EXERCIZE: Find a Way to translate trauma into humble compassion, instead of hiding from pain in apophenic dada[2] cadences. Break your addiction to the dreamy lights. Try to pierce the illusion and discover the universality behind this surreal kind of Nirvana experience. Crossing the "*Gate of the Gateless-Beyond*" is to embody all-out loss-for-words.
What do you believe in?

REVERSAL: ...and timeless time's Finding the Way and getting high for the wrong reasons like feedback when the song relapses and finally It becomes clear the anomalous mysteries of regular life always reincarnate viral cycles of full moon Darkness and a whole lotta bad trips and bad habits and cycles of bad parenting and bad judgment and bad Karma and a whole lotta regrets and, just maybe...
It's a whole lotta bullshit!

EXERCIZE: Find a Way to commune with this place through empathy. Challenge your dogma. Challenge my dogma. Who is the metaprogrammer?[2] Commitment is vital, fluidity is vital, service is vital, duality is singular. Meditate on this. Meditate without this. Believe in thought and action as echoes in eternity. Believe that "all is vanity[3]" as well.
Why do you persist?[4]

{ *Why speak questions on what's true?* }
$$\mathrm{I} = [(2 + 2 = 5) = (2 + 2 = 4)] = 0$$
("where music screams as *mu* ")

TRANSUBSTANTIATION.MXF

"I said of laughter, It is mad: and of mirth, What doeth it?"
- Eccl 2:2 KJV

Lo, Darkness, you're a laughing fuck
speed-dancing in the quantum phase
walking tall and without shame
within infinite and eternal change[1]
sex synthesis of Woe and pain
I arrange my atoms on the page

and I confess
this doesn't make sense
sense is a relic
of Father Time
and beyond belief
there's this beacon[2]
the Inn at the Oaks[3] abyss

here I confess
I've forgotten my name[4]
but no one knows everything
and maybe *the interstellar well of existence and being*
can make mistakes too
and it's no big deal, it's okay
there's almost something perfect about that

still I confess
I take a dive
through the doorless door
out of vain and rational self
transcending my whole reality shell
chaos invoking *mu* as well

once more, confess
I just don't know
how much further
yet to go
down the patient rabbit hole...
and I'm in love

CIRCUIT IV: BREAKING THROUGH THE PROGRAM'S INTERNAL LIGHT

TEMPLE_OF_THE_INEFFABLE.RAR

I dreamt a place
this healing space
an afterlife
of pure starlight
where sacred echoes
of the primal
tongue I can
no longer speak
still rang out clear
in empathy
a wild cleansing harmony
articulated heavenly
like peaceful whispers
through the trees
cherished family memories
my lives across the centuries
angelic romance fantasies
bright chants of prayer
camaraderie
a home for quantum circuitry
and all things lost
find new hope here
worshipped within
grandmother mirror
inversion of
the source of fear
words I could never
bear to hear
detethering behind my eyes
recasting secrets as benign
as Dark forever waved
goodbye

THE_COLLECTIVE_META-LORE.MP5

in my Dark web cry for help
decode a 10D[1] story shell
maybe a creation myth
uncovered breasts, the bardo well

in the desert
you can interpret your name[2]
in the trauma
you reincarnate your pain

bathwater oasis sings
sunlight mother![3] superstrings[4]
nursing kindness, pure wellspring
the Universe is this mirage thing

it's like *The Fountain* meets *The Ring*

#STOPSUICIDE.HEY

I'm not the center of the Universe
merely a temporary mouthpiece
and I don't deny pain
Jonathan Livingston Seagull[1]
maybe life's a joke we wouldn't get
but if only I could give you the moonlight[2]

I openly embrace you
you are as precious as the air in my lungs
more so than everything I've written or thought
or said or believed or sang
let yourself be valid
reach out to me[3] if you need a hand
make me understand

let me help to comprehend
for when I couldn't face my hurt
I dreamt of death
escaping through insanity
found relief through sleeping
in subconscious screaming fear
some little part of me was weeping
and yet, for now...
we're here

I'm only speaking
so keep breathing
ring in truths your diving bell
like living lantern essence shells
of bioluminescence
cleansing Darkness in the Well

DEADLIGHTS_IN_DARKNESS.BMP

like all red dreams do come to end
we bleed our trauma to transcend
our birth of shadow streetwise[1] sin
let me love, let me not exist

I am burning gaslight speed
glitching 'til I cease to be[2]
holy bardo echo fiend
cold and nude 'neath basement beams

as addict flesh in junky state
maybe I've bypassed this fate
Candyman, unmesh my soul
let me hope, please let me go

homeless time is screaming by
and I am cleansing slow
stare into life's deadlights
the tension lullaby may glow

I want to sing
with such frightening beauty
that no one else can
look away

SELF-REFERENTIAL_INVOCATION.ENC

"It turns out that an eerie type of chaos can lurk just behind a facade of order - and yet, deep inside the chaos lurks an even eerier type of order." - Douglas Hofstadter, Metamagical Themas: Questing for the Essence of Mind and Pattern

cut a deal with the Darkness
Find a Way to comprehend
the Middle[1] of poetic Zen
everything must end

what flesh we are that time transcends!
what is the next line or bend
but a melody we hum in rhyme?
what flesh we are that transcends time!

break the rhyme, break the 4th wall[2]
forgive myself
candlelight invocation calls
to close the abyss (doorway)

chant this final cleansing spell
I'm maybe reaching out as well
acknowledging
the depths of hurt
deconsecrate
my mother Earth
ascending from the depths of hell
Father Time within the mesh
chant this final cleansing spell
tattoo *mu* upon my flesh

but this is not an exit[3]
or a punchline to some joke
it's my honest attempt to extract
some patience, wellness, and music

from this eerily
familiar
Malware

APPENDIX

.zip - Compressed file format used for archiving larger amounts of data into a smaller package for later extraction. Created in 1989 by Phillip Katz.

.php - Dynamic webpage file format. Abbreviation of "personal home page" in this context.

.cmd - Imperative batch file format from Microsoft/DOS/IBM programming languages for series of executable commands.

.psd - Desktop publishing file format for Adobe's Photoshop software. Dates back to Thomas and John Knoll in 1987. Includes layers, masks, and transparency.

.exe - Executable file format dating back to 1985. While often used for installing programs, the format is also traditionally the most common format for malware and computer viruses.

.logic - Audio project format from Apple's digital audio workstation (DAW) and MIDI sequencer program. Initial release: 1993 (as Notator Logic), bought by Apple in 2002.

.jpg - Common image format. Abbreviation of Joint Photographic Experts Group.

.rom - Format associated with video game storage media. Abbreviation of read-only memory. Often associated with emulators, programs designed to "emulate" or copy older gaming systems through a PC or mobile device.

.gif - Image format developed by CompuServe in 1987. In popular consciousness, the format is associated with short, perpetually looping animations.

.sim - File format for Steam backup information. Steam is a video game distribution service launched by Valve Software in 2003.

.meta - File format associated with certain types of metadata. Metadata is data about data.

.wav - Lossless uncompressed audio format developed by Microsoft and IBM.

.mp4 - Compressed video and audio file format. Introduced in 1998.

.png - High-quality image file format. Abbreviation of Portable Network Graphics.

.html - HyperText Markup Language. The standard scripting/markup language for web processing.

.mXf - Material Exchange Format.

.rar - Compressed archive file format developed by Eugene Roshal in 1993. These files have uses similar to .zip files and usually can be extracted via the same programs.

.mps - Mathematical Programming System file format.

.key - In this context, file format for Keynote Presentation files.

.bmp - Bitmap image format.

.enc - Encoded file format.

FOOTNOTES

INDEX_PASSAGE.PHP:

1. **Apophenia:** A mental disorder characterized by perception of patterns and synchronicities that do not really exist. The author takes issue with the metaphysical claims this necessarily implies.

2. **Rabbit hole:** See *Alice's Adventures in Wonderland*, the 1865 novel by Lewis Carroll. The rabbit hole is the portal through which Alice enters another world in the first chapter. The term "going down the rabbit hole" now carries the connotation of getting carried away exploring conspiracies and mysteries, especially online.

3. **Eight Circuit Model of Human Consciousness:** Theoretical model for understanding human consciousness developed by Timothy Leary and expounded upon by Robert Anton Wilson. Wilson described the eighth and final circuit as the "non-local quantum circuit."

4. **Mu:** Japanese word for "not" or "not have", this term has significance in Zen Buddhist teachings. Phillip Toshio Sudo described it in *Zen Guitar* as a "timeless void transcending rational comprehension" and "the barrier at the end of thinking, where logic can go no further."

DREAM_OF_THIS_TALEK.CMD:

0. **Talek:** A recursive architecture within dreams resembling a hellish prison where escape, even

through death, is impossible. Or a doorway. Or whatever you need it to be.

1. **Sunken Place:** See *Get Out,* a 2017 horror film directed by Jordan Peele. Void of consciousness induced by hypnosis.

2. **Mad Hatter:** See *Alice's Adventures in Wonderland,* the 1865 novel by Lewis Carroll. Though he is never actually referred to by this name in the book, the title has entered popular consciousness. He is being punished by time in an eternal tea party.

3. **Bardo:** In some sects of Buddhism, a state between death and rebirth. This is where the soul resides between reincarnations. It is said that the bardo can be a terrifying place.

4. **Black Mirror: Bandersnatch:** An interactive movie released via Netflix in 2019. The movie is a choose-your-own-adventure experience that breaks the fourth wall.

CORRUPTED_PROGRAMMING.EXE:

1. **The Shawshank Redemption:** A 1994 prison drama film directed by Frank Darabont.

2. **Pied Piper of Hamelin:** A German folk legend dating back to the Middle Ages. The Pied Piper was hired to lure rats away from the town. When the townsfolk refused to pay him for his services, he led the children of the town away.

3. **The Fountain:** A 2006 film by Darren Aronofsky. The content and style comprises a unique blend of fantasy, spirituality, romance, and science fiction.

4. **The Ring:** A 2002 horror film directed by Gore
   Verbinski. Though it is an Americanized remake of a
   1998 Japanese film, the author contends that this
   version is actually scarier.

5. **Trojan:** A type of malware that masquerades as another
   file to gain access to sensitive data and corrupt it. The
   name is a reference to the story of the Trojan horse in
   Greek mythology.

6. **Shoney's:** See *Rick and Morty* S3, E1 ("The Rickshank
   Rickdemption"). A trick, a fabricated origin story used
   to upload a virus. "We never left his Shoney's!"

NARAKA.LOGIC:

0. **Naraka:** Realm of punishment and torment in some
   sects of Hinduism, Buddhism, and Jainism. Imperfectly
   analogous to the Hells of the Abrahamic religions.

1. **Yama:** Hindu and Buddhist god of death. His name
   means "twin" in Sanskrit.

2. **Gooseprickles:** Colloquial term for the bumps that form
   on human skin as reflex to fear, intense excitement, or
   arousal. Other names for the phenomena include
   goosebumps, heebie-jeebies, and horripilation.

PORTRAIT_OF_CIRCADIA.JPG:

0. **Circadia:** The looping universe in which we are
   currently existing.

1. **Circumpunct:** The lost symbol of the system from the
   outside. God, eternity, the sun.
The void escaping my dreams on a floppy disk for you.

2. **Zenith:** The time something is at its most powerful. The top of the celestial sphere in astronomy. Also, an American Electronics company founded in 1918, known for developing the television remote control.

NOTHING_IS_REAL.GIF:

0. **Boards of Canada - Nothing is Real** (from 2013's *Tomorrow's Harvest)*

1. **Transmigration:** In some religions, transmigration is the process of the soul moving from one existence to another after death. This process supposedly represents an endless cycle.

2. **DeepDream:** A Google computer vision program designed to create a dream-like appearance in images through over-processing.

3. **Enter the Void:** A 2009 experimental art film directed by Gaspar Noe. Explores the bardo experience in harrowing first-person detail.

4. **Candyman:** A 1992 supernatural horror film directed by Bernard Rose.

THE_GRAND_ILLUSION_AS_GODOT.SIM:

0[a]. **The Grand Illusion:** See *Rick and Morty* S3 E7 ("The Ricklantis Mixup").

0[b]. **Waiting for Godot:** An absurdist/existentialist play by Samuel Beckett, premiered in English in 1953.

1. **I Have No Mouth and I Must Scream:** Science fiction/horror short story by Harlan Ellison, published in 1967. Iconic and essential to understanding.

ANYTHING_OUTSIDE.META:

1. **The Gateless Barrier:** Collection of 48 Zen koans compiled by the 13th century Chinese Zen master Wumen Huikai. Koans may be described as poetic riddles or paradoxes designed as a gateway to enlightenment for students of Zen teachings. Or they may be described otherwise. The issue of how to accurately describe koans still sees heavy debate online and elsewhere at the time of writing. However, the first and arguably most famous koan in the collection is the "Mu koan". Allegedly, this koan led to Wumen Huikai's own enlightenment.

2. **Time is a flat circle:** See *True Detective* S1, E5 ("The Secret Fate of All Life"). This idea is synonymous with eternal return.

3. **Robert Anton Wilson Explains Everything (or, Old Bob Exposes His Ignorance):** An enlightening and funny audiobook collection of the man himself giving interviews and lectures on everything from poetry, literature, and history to psychedelic drugs, consciousness, and conspiracies. Originally released in 2001.

CELESTIAL_SPAM.WAV:

1. **Frank Zappa - Cosmik Debris** (From 1974's *Apostrophe*)

2. **Drinking the Kool-Aid:** A reference here to the Peoples Temple mass murder/suicide in Jonestown, Guyana in 1978. The phrase now holds the meaning of buying into the dangerous ideology of a cult.

3. **Proverbs:** Book of wisdom and moral teachings in the Hebrew bible and the Christian Old Testament. Attributed to Solomon, King of Israel.

A_SONG_OF_SILENCE.MP4:

1. **Eris:** Greek goddess of strife and discord. Worship of Eris is advocated in the Principia Discordia, a religious paradigm developed by Malaclypse the Younger and Lord Omar. Popularized and expanded upon by Robert Anton Wilson.

2. **Samsara:** The karmic cycle of death and rebirth in the Dharmic religions.

EMPTY_CUP_METAPHOR.PNG:

0. **Carrying an empty cup:** A saying that comes from a Zen parable about a scholar who was too full of his own ideas to learn. The essence is that you must carry an empty cup for anyone to be able to fill it.

1. **Sunyata:** A Buddhist concept illustrating that all of reality is empty of intrinsic existence and nature. Understanding sunyata is part of the journey one takes via Buddhism.

ZENSANITY_MADE_SIMPLE.HTML:

1. **2 + 2 = 5:** Equation published in George Orwell's 1949 dystopian novel, *Nineteen Eighty-Four.* It proves crucial to understanding the novel's central conceit of doublethink.

2. **Dada:** Avant-garde art movement, originating in early 20th century Europe. Dada works seem primarily concerned with rejecting logic and reason (and often traditional aesthetic principles). The movement eventually extended beyond visual art to music, poetry, and film.

3. **All is Vanity:** Reference to the Old Testament book of Ecclesiastes. Traditionally attributed to King Solomon of Israel, though this has been disputed. This book is a rare moment in the Bible in which the author heavily questions the meaning of life, even a life lived for God.

4. **Why do you persist?:** See *The Matrix Revolutions,* a 2003 sci-fi/action film directed by the Wachowskis.

TRANSUBSTANTIATION.MXF:

1. **Infinite and Eternal Change:** See Aleister Crowley's "The Testament of Magdalen Blair", a horror short story first published in 1913.

2. **Beacon:** See *The Sopranos* S6A, E2 ("Join the Club"). The tower of the dead, the source of the cosmic architecture, the wellspring of truth.

3. **Inn at the Oaks:** See *The Sopranos*, S6A, E3 ("Mayham"). The entrance to the void, the exit from life, the reunion with infinity.

4. **Ego death:** Complete loss of self-identity, usually temporary. The term was used by Timothy Leary in reference to transcendent psychedelic experiences. Though some dispute the validity and value of using substances like LSD or psilocybin mushrooms to reach this state, the same conditions may also arise from dedicated meditation practice and/or dream yoga.

THE_COLLECTIVE_META-LORE.MP5:

1. **Tenth Dimension:** In some schools of string theory, a specialized field of theory within physics, the universe exists within ten dimensions, with the tenth dimension as the highest plane of hyperspace.

2. **America - A Horse with No Name** (From 1971's *America*)

3. **mother!:** A 2017 horror film directed by Darren Aronofsky. Features strong allegorical, biblical, and mythic elements. Some interpret the mother as sympathy for Satan.

4. **Supersymmetry/M-Theory:** Overarching unification theory of the universe conjectured by American theoretical physicist Edward Witten in 1995. The "M" in M-theory can stand for magic, mystery, or membrane, and should be viewed as a stand in until a more accurate title is decided upon. Michio Kaku, another theoretical physicist, once described the vibrations of tenth dimensional superstrings creating all of reality as a form of cosmic music.

#STOPSUICIDE.KEY:

0. **#StopSuicide:** Hashtag put forth by the American Foundation for Suicide Prevention to advocate for research, education, and support to better arm the public and mental health professionals alike to help those who are in need.

1. **Jonathan Livingston Seagull:** A spiritual book by Richard Bach. Published in 1970.

2. **If only I could give him the moon:** A Zen parable about the monk Ryokan, who, when discovering a thief in his

bare, ascetic hut, offered the robe from his own back to the man. The thief left in shame. Ryokan wished he could have given him the moon.

3. **Me:** metaselfmusic@gmail.com

DEADLIGHTS_IN_DARKNESS.BMP:

0. **Deadlights:** The hypnotic and destructive orange lights that make up the core of the shape-shifting alien entity Pennywise, from Stephen King's 1986 horror novel, *It.*

1. **The Shadowy Street:** A 1931 surreal horror short story by French author Jean Ray.

2. **Become So Shining That We Cease to Be:** A 1991 short story by the prolific American writer Chelsea Quinn Yarbro.

SELF-REFERENTIAL_INVOCATION.ENC:

0. **The Middle Way:** A path taught by Siddhartha Gautama (the Buddha), advocating balance between indulgence and abstinence. Through his own life experiences, he came to understand that neither extreme was conducive to a right and liberated life.

1. **The Fourth Wall:** Convention originating within the theater of not directly acknowledging the audience, as if a "fourth wall" were present between the stage and the seats. Breaking the fourth wall can occur in other media as well, including in books. An example might be if the author were to say, "Hi reader, this is Dylan Sonderman here, the author of Lucid_Malware.zip: Poems of Broken Programming, the poetry book you're currently reading (and hopefully enjoying!)"

2. **This is not an exit:** The final line from Bret Easton Ellis's 1991 transgressive horror novel, *American Psycho.* The work has proved itself essential and truly prophetic in more ways than one, but the ending, as the line implies, is not a "real ending" at all. There is no catharsis. Life goes on, until it doesn't. In the meantime...

THANKS

Lizzy, Chad Lutz, Rebecca Pilar, Alex Pica, Nick Baronzzi, Olivia, Samantha Wightman, Taylor Hertz, Joseph Pica, Marion Rucker IV, Treyce Jacks, Seth Holt, Nick Chiudioni, Diana Pica, Toni Ponzo, Kathryn Young, Brad Warner, Drew B. David, Maudlin House, Bud Smith, Ted Lyons, Katherine Orr, Tom Saal, Kim Winebrenner, Charles Little, Robert Anton Wilson, American Psycho, Thomas Ligotti, Lil Ugly Mane, Emily Dickinson, Teddy Roosevelt, Darren Aronofsky, Black Mirror, George Carlin, James Joyce, Kendrick Lamar, Henry Rollins, Nintendo, House of Leaves, Pikes Peak, HP Lovecraft, Wikipedia, Obi-Wan Kenobi, The Third Policeman, Darren Shan, Mindless Self Indulgence, Harlan Ellison, Tracy Denholm, Robert Greene, Ron at Sopranos Autopsy, Stephen King, Blood Meridian, Luna Lovegood, Rick and Morty, Dogen, Christian O'Keeffe, Philip Toshio Sudo, Norman Mailer, Christopher Paolini, Marge Piercy, David Chase, If On A Winter's Night a Traveler, Cedric Bixler-Zavala, Kayo Dot, Christopher Hitchens, Alexis Kale, Nick Courtright, and Patrick Sonderman.

ABOUT ATMOSPHERE PRESS

Atmosphere Press is an independent, full-service publisher for excellent books in all genres and for all audiences. Learn more about what we do at atmospherepress.com.

We encourage you to check out some of Atmosphere's latest releases, which are available at Amazon.com and via order from your local bookstore:

Report from the Sea of Moisture, poetry by Stuart Jay Silverman

White Snake Diary, nonfiction by Jane P. Perry

From Rags to Rags, essays by Ellie Guzman

The Enemy of Everything, poetry by Michael Jones

Giving Up the Ghost, essays by Tina Cabrera

The Stargazers, poetry by James McKee

The Pretend Life, poetry by Michelle Brooks

Minnesota and Other Poems, poetry by Daniel N. Nelson

Interviews from the Last Days, sci-fi poetry by Christina Loraine

Unorthodoxy, a novel by Joshua A.H. Harris

the oneness of Reality, poetry by Brock Mehler

Drop Dead Red, poetry by Elizabeth Carmer

Aging Without Grace, poetry by Sandra Fox Murphy

No Home Like a Raft, poetry by Martin Jon Porter

Adrift, poetry by Kristy Peloquin

ABOUT THE AUTHOR

Dylan Sonderman writes poetry, science fiction, and horror when he is not composing or playing music. Born in Akron, OH in 1990, he attended Kent State University and earned a BA in English with a minor in Writing. In his free time, he enjoys video games, cooking, and meditation. Dylan lives in Cleveland with his wife, Elizabeth, and their two dogs, Gertie and Ozzy. His music is available under his own name and under the name Metaself. *Lucid_Malware.zip* is his debut book of poetry.

Everything Mirrors the Void

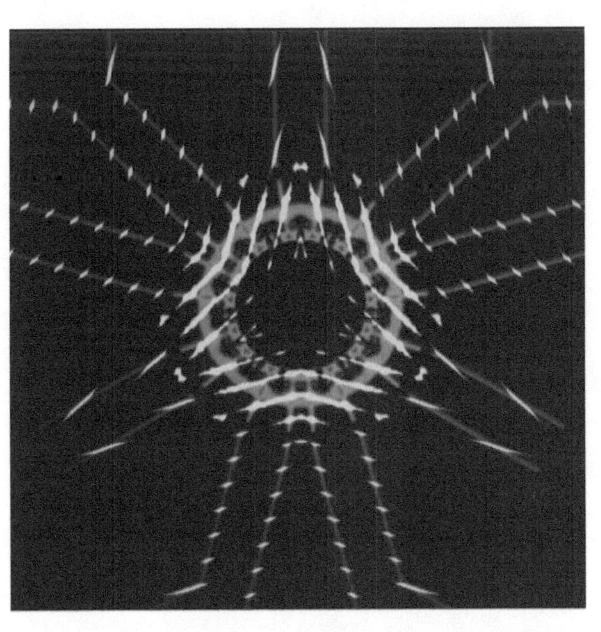

www.ingramcontent.com/pod-product-compliance
Lightning Source LLC
Chambersburg PA
CBHW032127050726
47590CB00008B/3001